The Crisis of Narration

T0056588

Byung-Chul Han

The Crisis of Narration

Translated by Daniel Steuer

polity

Originally published in German as *Die Krise der Narration* © MSB Matthes & Seitz Berlin Verlagsgesellschaft mbH, Berlin 2023. All rights reserved.

This English edition © Polity Press, 2024

Excerpt from Peter Handke, *Zwiegespräch* © Suhrkamp Verlag AG, Berlin, 2022. Included with permission of the publisher.

Polity Press
65 Bridge Street
Cambridge CB2 1UR, UK

Polity Press
111 River Street
Hoboken, NJ 07030, USA

All rights reserved. Except for the quotation of short passages for the purpose of criticism and review, no part of this publication may be reproduced, stored in a retrieval system or transmitted, in any form or by any means, electronic, mechanical, photocopying, recording or otherwise, without the prior permission of the publisher.

ISBN-13: 978-1-5095-6042-4 – hardback
ISBN-13: 978-1-5095-6043-1 – paperback

A catalogue record for this book is available from the British Library.

Library of Congress Control Number: 2023939907

Typeset in 11pt on 15pt Janson Text
by Cheshire Typesetting Ltd, Cuddington, Cheshire
Printed and bound in Great Britain by CPI Group (UK) Ltd, Croydon

The publisher has used its best endeavours to ensure that the URLs for external websites referred to in this book are correct and active at the time of going to press. However, the publisher has no responsibility for the websites and can make no guarantee that a site will remain live or that the content is or will remain appropriate.

Every effort has been made to trace all copyright holders, but if any have been overlooked the publisher will be pleased to include any necessary credits in any subsequent reprint or edition.

For further information on Polity, visit our website:
politybooks.com

Contents

Watch out, narration.
A little bit of patience for narration, please.
And then: patience through narration!

Peter Handke*

* *Zwiegespräch*, Frankfurt am Main: Suhrkamp, 2022, p. 10

PREFACE

Everyone is talking about 'narratives'. Paradoxically, the inflation of narrative betrays a crisis of narration. At the heart of all the noise of storytelling, there is a narrative vacuum that expresses itself in a lack of meaning and orientation.[1] Neither storytelling nor the narrative turn will be able to bring about the *return of narration*. A paradigm becomes a topic, and a fashionable object of academic research, only when there is a *deep-seated alienation* from it. All the talk about narratives suggests their dysfunctionality.

As long as narratives were our anchor in *being*, that is, as long as they provided us with a *site*, turning being-in-the-world into being-at-home by furnishing life with meaning, support and orientation – in other words, as long as living was a *narrating* – there was never any talk of storytelling or narration. The inflation in the use of such concepts begins precisely when narratives lose their original power, their gravitational force, their secret and magic. Once they are seen as something *constructed*, they lose their moment of *inner truth*. They are considered contingent, exchangeable and modifiable. They are no longer the source of what is binding, of what unites. They no longer anchor us in *being*. Despite the present hype around narratives, we live in a *post-narrative time*. Narrative consciousness, allegedly rooted in the human brain, is a conception that is possible only in a post-narrative time, that is, outside of the narrative spell.

Religion is a typical narrative with an inner moment of truth. It *narrates* contingency away. Christian religion is a meta-narrative that reaches into every nook and cranny of life and anchors it in being. Time itself becomes freighted with narrative. In the Christian calendar, each day is meaningful. In the post-narrative era, the calendar is de-narrativized; it becomes a meaningless schedule of appointments. Religious holidays are highlights and high points of a narrative. Without a narrative, there are no festivities, no festive times – no festive moods with their intensified feeling of being. All that is left are work and free time, production and consumption. In the post-narrative era, festivities are commercialized. They become events and spectacles. Rituals are also narrative practices: they are always embedded in a narrative context. As symbolic techniques for creating enclosure, they transform being-in-the-world into a being-at-home.

A world-changing and world-opening narrative cannot be created by the whim of a single person. Rather, it owes its existence to a complex process in which various forces and actors are involved. Ultimately, a narrative is an *expression of the mood of a time*. Such narratives, which have an *inner moment of truth*, are the opposite of the eviscerated, exchangeable and contingent narratives – that is, the micro-narratives – of the present, which lack *gravity*, which lack any *moment of truth*.

Narration is a *concluding form*. It creates a *closed* order that founds meaning and identity. In late modernity, which is characterized by opening up and unbounding, forms of concluding and closing off are increasingly eroded. At the same time, with increasing permissiveness comes a growing need for narrative forms of closure. Populist, nationalist and right-wing extremist or tribal narratives, including conspiracy theories, cater to this need. They are taken up because they *offer meaning and identity*. However, in the post-narrative era, with its intensifying experience of contingency, these narratives do not have any strong binding force.

Narratives create a community. Storytelling, by contrast, brings forth only a fleeting community – the commodified form of community. These communities consist of consumers. No amount of storytelling could recreate the fire around which humans gather to tell each other stories. That fire has long since burnt out. It has been replaced by the digital screen, which separates people as individual consumers. Consumers are lonely. They do not form a community. Nor can the 'stories' shared on social media fill the narrative vacuum. They are merely forms of pornographic self-presentation or self-promotion. Posting, liking and sharing content are consumerist practices that intensify the narrative crisis.

Through storytelling, capitalism appropriates the narrative and submits it to consumption. Storytelling produces narratives in a consumable form. It charges products with emotion. It promises unique experiences. We buy, sell and consume narratives and emotions. *Stories sell. Storytelling is storyselling.*

Narration and information are counteracting forces. Information intensifies the experience of contingency, whereas narration reduces it by turning the accidental into necessity. Information lacks the *solidity of being*. Niklas Luhmann puts it lucidly: '[Information's] cosmology is not a cosmology of being but of contingency.'[2] *Being* and *information* are mutually exclusive. A *lack of being*, a *forgetfulness of being*, is thus immanent to the information society. Information is additive and cumulative. It is not a bearer of sense, whereas a narration carries sense. The original meaning of 'sense' is direction. Today, we are perfectly informed, but we lack orientation. Information also dissects time into a mere sequence of present moments. A narrative, by contrast, brings forth a temporal continuum, that is, a *story*.

On the one hand, the informatization of society accelerates its de-narrativization. On the other, amid the tsunami of information, there arises a need for meaning, identity and orientation, that is, a need *to clear the thick forest of information in which we risk losing ourselves*. The flood of ephemeral narratives, including conspiracy theories, and the tsunami of information are ultimately two sides of the same coin. Adrift in the sea of information and data, we seek a *narrative anchor*.

We tell fewer and fewer stories in our everyday lives. Telling stories is in decline because communication takes the form of the exchange of information. Scarcely any stories are told on social media. Stories unite people by promoting their capacity for empathy. They create genuine community. The loss of empathy in the age of the smartphone is a clear sign that this technology is not a medium for telling stories. Its technical dispositif is already a barrier to the telling of stories. Typing and swiping are not narrative gestures. A smartphone allows only for the accelerated exchange of information. Narrating presupposes close listening and deep attention. The narrative community is a community of attentive listeners. But we increasingly lack the patience for attentive listening, even the patience for narrative.

When everything becomes contingent, fleeting and accidental, and all that is binding and unifying dissolves – that is, in the current storm of contingency – there is a clamour for storytelling. The inflation of narrative betrays a need to be able to cope with contingency. But storytelling is unable to transform the information society, which is devoid of orientation and meaning, back into a stable narrative community. Rather, storytelling is a pathological phenomenon of our era. The narrative crisis has a long prehistory. This essay attempts to trace it.

From Narration to Information

The founder of the French daily newspaper *Le Figaro*, Hippolyte de Villemessant, expressed the essence of information in the following remark: 'To my readers, an attic fire in the Latin Quarter is more important than a revolution in Madrid.' For Walter Benjamin, the remark 'makes strikingly clear that what gets the readiest hearing is no longer intelligence coming from afar, but the information which supplies a handle for what is nearest'. The newspaper reader's attention extends only to what is near. It *shrinks* to mere curiosity. The modern newspaper reader jumps from one news item to the next, instead of letting her gaze drift into the distance and linger. The modern reader has lost *the long, slow, lingering gaze*.

A piece of news that is embedded in a *story* has an altogether different spatial and temporal structure from that of information. It comes 'from afar'.[1] This *distance* is its characteristic trait. Modernity is characterized by the progressive demolition of farness, the place of which is taken by gaplessness. Information is a genuine expression of a gaplessness that makes everything available. A piece of news that arrives is marked by an *unavailable distance*. It announces a historical event that resists availability and computability. We are at its mercy, as if faced with the *power of destiny*.

Information does not survive the moment it is registered: 'It lives only at that moment; it has to surrender to it completely and explain itself to it without losing any time.'[2] Unlike information, a piece of news possesses a temporal breadth through which it is related to *what is to come* beyond the present moment. It is *pregnant with history*. A broad narrative *oscillation* inheres in it.

Information is the medium of *reporters* who sift the world for news. The *storyteller* [Erzähler] is the reporter's counter-figure. A storyteller does not inform or explain. In fact, the art of storytelling demands that information be withheld: 'Actually, it is half the art of storytelling [Erzählen] to keep a story free from explanation as one recounts it.'[3] Withheld information – that is, a lack of explanation – heightens narrative tension.

Gaplessness destroys nearness as well as distance. Nearness is not the same as gaplessness, because distance is inscribed in nearness. Nearness and distance cause and animate each other. It is this interplay between nearness and distance that creates the *aura*: 'The trace is appearance of a nearness, however far removed the thing that left it behind may be. The aura is appearance of a distance, however close the thing that calls it forth.'[4] The aura is *narrative* because it is *impregnated by distance*. By removing distance, information, by contrast, de-auratizes and disenchants the world. It *fixates* the world and thus makes it available. The 'trace' that points to the distance is full of allusions; it *tempts us to narrate*.

The cause of the narrative crisis in modernity is the deluge of information. The spirit of narration is suffocated by the flood. Benjamin states: 'If the art of storytelling has become rare, the dissemination of information has played a decisive role in this state of affairs.'[5] Information pushes to the margins those events that cannot be explained but only narrated. A narrative often has something wondrous and mysterious around its edges. It is incompatible with information, which represents the opposite of the secret. Explanation and narration are mutually exclusive:

> Every morning brings us news from across the globe, yet we are poor in noteworthy stories. This is because nowadays no event comes to us without already being shot through with explanations. In other words, by now almost nothing that happens benefits storytelling; almost everything benefits information.[6]

For Benjamin, Herodotus is the ancient master of narration. His story of Psammenitus serves as the prime example of his art of narration. When the Egyptian king was captured following his defeat at the hands of the Persian king Cambyses, Cambyses humbled his prisoner by forcing him to watch the triumphal procession of the Persians. He arranged it that the prisoner should see his captured daughter pass by as a maid. While all the Egyptians standing along the way were lamenting this fact, Psammenitus stood silent and motionless, his eyes fixed on the ground. When he saw his son, who was being led to his execution as part of the procession, he was still motionless. But when he recognized his servant, an old and frail man, among the prisoners, he hit his head with his fists and expressed his deep mourning. For Benjamin, this story reveals what true storytelling is. He believes that any attempt to explain why the Egyptian king began to lament only when he saw his servant would destroy the narrative tension. Forgoing explanation is essential to true storytelling. Narrative does without explanation:

> Herodotus offers no explanations. His report is utterly dry. That is why, after thousands of years, this story from ancient Egypt is still capable of provoking astonishment and reflection. It is like those seeds of grain that have lain for centuries in the airtight chambers of the pyramids and have retained their germinative power to this day.[7]

According to Benjamin, a story 'does not expend itself. It preserves and concentrates its energy and is capable of releasing it even after a long time.'[8] The temporality of information is altogether different. It is relevant only briefly, so it is quickly exhausted. It is effective only for a moment. Bits of information are like specks of dust, not seeds of grain. They lack germinal force. Once they are registered, they immediately sink into oblivion, like answerphone messages once they have been listened to.

For Benjamin, the earliest sign of the decline of narration is the rise of the novel at the beginning of modernity. A narrative feeds off experience and passes it down from one generation to the next. 'The storyteller takes what he tells from experience – his own or that reported by others. And he in turn makes it the experience of those who are listening to his tale.' A novel, by contrast, is an expression of the 'profound perplexity of the living'.[9] A narrative creates community; a novel, however, is born of the lonely, isolated individual. A novel psychologizes and interprets, but a narrative proceeds descriptively: 'The most extraordinary things, marvelous things, are related with the greatest accuracy, but the psychological connections among the events are not forced on the reader.' However, the ultimate decline of narration comes not with the novel but with the rise of information under capitalism:

> On the other hand, we can see that with the complete ascendancy of the bourgeoisie – which in fully developed capitalism has the press as one of its most important instruments – a form of communication emerges which, no matter how ancient its origins, never before decisively influenced the epic form. But now it does exert such an influence. And ultimately it confronts storytelling as no less of a stranger than did the novel . . . This new form of communication is information.[10]

Storytelling requires a state of relaxation. For Benjamin, the 'apogee of mental relaxation' is boredom. It is the 'dream bird that hatches the egg of experience'.[11] It is 'a warm gray fabric lined on the inside with the most lustrous and colorful of silks. In this fabric we wrap ourselves when we dream.'[12] Noisy information – the 'rustling in the leaves' – drives the dream bird away. Amid the murmur of the press, there can be 'no more weaving and spinning',

5

only the production and consumption of information as stimuli.[13]

Narrating and listening foster each other. The narrative community is a *community of careful listeners*. A particular kind of attention is inherent to careful listening. People who listen carefully are oblivious to themselves; they immerse *themselves* in what they hear: 'The more self-forgetful the listener is, the more deeply what he listens to is impressed upon his memory.'[14] We are increasingly losing the gift to listen carefully. We *play to the gallery*; we *eavesdrop on each other* instead of forgetting ourselves and listening intensely.

On the internet, this space of *rustling digital leaves*, the dream bird cannot build a nest. The information seekers drive him away. In today's state of hyperactivity, where boredom is not allowed to emerge, we never reach the state of deep mental relaxation. The information society is an age of *heightened mental tension*, because the essence of information is surprise and the stimulus it provides. The tsunami of information means that our perceptual apparatus is permanently stimulated. It can no longer enter into contemplation. The tsunami of information fragments our attention. It prevents the contemplative lingering that is essential to narrating and careful listening.

Digitalization sets in train a process that Benjamin could not have foreseen. He associates information with the press, and for him the press is a form of communication alongside the narrative and the novel. In the process of digitalization, however, information acquires an altogether different status. *Reality itself takes on the form of information and data.* For the most part, we perceive reality

6

in terms of information or through the lens of information. Information is an idea – that is, a re-presentation. When reality takes the form of information, the immediate *experience of presence* withers. When digitalization gives everything the form of information, reality is flattened.

A century after Benjamin, information is becoming a *new form of being*, even a *new form of domination*. Alongside neoliberalism, we are seeing the establishment of an information regime that works not through repression but through seduction. It takes on a *smart* form. It does not operate through imperatives or prohibitions. It does not silence us. Rather, this smart form of domination constantly asks us to communicate our opinions, needs and preferences, to tell our lives, to post, share and like messages. Freedom is not repressed but comprehensively exploited. It turns into control and manipulation. Because it does not need to appear, smart domination is highly efficient. It hides behind the illusion of freedom and communication. By posting, sharing and liking, we subordinate ourselves to the context of domination.

The rush of information and communication is stupefying. We are no longer masters of our communication; rather, we are subject to an accelerated exchange of information that escapes our conscious control. Communication is increasingly controlled by external forces. It seems to be guided by an automatic, mechanical process that is directed by algorithms, a process of which we are, however, unaware. We are at the mercy of the algorithmic black box. Human beings are reduced to data sets that can be controlled and exploited.

In the information regime, Georg Büchner's remark is still relevant: 'We are puppets, our strings are pulled by unknown forces, we ourselves are nothing, nothing!'[15] The only difference is that the forces guiding us today are so subtle and hidden that we are no longer aware of them. We even confuse them with freedom. Charlie Kaufman's puppet animation *Anomalisa* illustrates the logic of smart domination. It depicts a world in which all humans look alike and speak with the same voice. This world reveals the neoliberal hell of the same, in which, paradoxically, there are constant invocations of authenticity and creativity. The film's protagonist, Michael Stone, is a successful motivational coach. One day, he suddenly realizes that he is a puppet. The mouth falls off his face, and he holds it in his hands. He is stunned: the mouth continues to chatter all by itself.

The Poverty of Experience

Walter Benjamin begins his essay 'Experience and Poverty' with the fable of the old man who, on his death-bed, tells his sons that there is a treasure buried in his vineyard. The sons dig every day, across the whole vineyard, but find no treasure. When autumn comes, they realize that their father had passed on a piece of experience: 'the blessing lies in hard work and not in gold'. For the vineyard provided a richer harvest than any other in the country. Experience is characterized by the fact that it is passed down from one generation to the next through *narration*. Benjamin laments the loss of experience in modernity:

> Where has it all gone? Who still meets people who really know how to tell a story? Where do you still hear words from the dying that last, and that pass from one

generation to the next like a precious ring? Who can still call on a proverb when he needs one?[1]

Communicable experience passed on by word of mouth is becoming increasingly rare. Nothing is passed down; nothing is narrated.

Benjamin holds that the storyteller 'is a man who has counsel for his listeners'.[2] Such counsel does not simply provide solutions to problems. Rather, it suggests how *a story is to be continued*. The one seeking counsel and the counsellor both belong to a narrative community. Those seeking counsel must themselves be able to *narrate*. In real life, counsel is sought and given in a narrative context. As wisdom, it is 'woven into the fabric of real life'.[3] Wisdom is embedded in *life as narrative*. If life can no longer be narrated, wisdom deteriorates, and its place is taken by *problem-solving techniques*. Wisdom is *narrated truth*: 'The art of storytelling is nearing its end because the epic side of truth, wisdom, is dying out.'[4]

Experience requires tradition and continuity. Experience stabilizes life and makes the narration of life possible. When experience disintegrates, when there is no longer anything binding or stable, all that is left is *bare life*, a kind of *survival*. Benjamin expresses his scepticism towards modernity and its poverty of experience in unequivocal terms. For him, it

is obvious: experience has fallen in value . . . A generation that had gone to school on horsedrawn streetcars now stood under the open sky in a landscape where nothing remained unchanged but the clouds and, beneath those

10

clouds, in a force field of destructive torrents and explosions, the tiny, fragile human body.[5]

Despite his doubts, Benjamin frequently reveals some – limited – optimism regarding modernity. His tone often switches from the elegiac to the euphoric. He also believes that he can see a 'new beauty' in the vanishing of experience. He grants that the poverty of experience is a new form of barbarism, but claims that something positive can be found in it: 'Barbarism? Yes, indeed. We say this in order to introduce a new, positive concept of barbarism. For what does poverty of experience do for the barbarian?'[6]

Experience founds a historical continuum. The new barbarians emancipate themselves from the context of tradition in which experience is embedded. The poverty of experience forces the barbarians 'to start from scratch'. They are animated by the *passion of the new*. They begin with a tabula rasa. They see themselves not as storytellers but as 'constructors'. Benjamin generalizes the new barbarianism and turns it into the *principle of the new*: 'Such a constructor was Descartes, who required nothing more to launch his entire philosophy than the single certitude, "I think, therefore I am." And he went on from there.'[7]

The new barbarians celebrate the poverty of experience as a moment of emancipation:

Poverty of experience. This should not be understood to mean that people are yearning for new experience. No, they long to free themselves from experience; they long for a world in which they can make such pure and decided use of their poverty – their outer poverty, and ultimately also their inner poverty – that it will lead to something respectable.[8]

Benjamin lists a number of modern artists and writers who affirm the poverty of experience and harbour no illusions about it. They are inspired by 'starting from the very beginning'.[9] They are determined to bid farewell to the fusty world of the bourgeoisie and 'turn instead to the naked man of the contemporary world who lies screaming like a newborn babe in the dirty diapers of the present'.[10] They commit themselves to transparency and reject anything secretive, that is, anything auratic. They also reject anything to do with humanism. Benjamin points out that they like to give their children 'dehumanized' names such as 'Peka', 'Labu' or 'Aviakhim' – the name of an airline. For Benjamin, Paul Scheerbart's glass house is emblematic of the future life of human beings:

> It is no coincidence that glass is such a hard, smooth material to which nothing can be fixed. A cold and sober material into the bargain. Objects made of glass have no 'aura'. Glass is, in general, the enemy of secrets.[11]

Benjamin also counts Mickey Mouse among the new barbarians:

> Tiredness is followed by sleep, and then it is not uncommon for a dream to make up for the sadness and discouragement of the day – a dream that shows us in its realized form the simple but magnificent existence for which the energy is lacking in reality. The existence of Mickey Mouse is such a dream for contemporary man.[12]

Benjamin admires the lightness that characterizes Mickey Mouse's existence. Mickey Mouse becomes a figure of salvation who re-enchants the world:

> And people who have grown weary of the endless complications of everyday living and to whom the purpose of existence seems to have been reduced to the most distant vanishing point on an endless horizon, are redeemed by the sight of an existence . . . in which a car is no heavier than a straw hat and the fruit on the tree becomes round as quickly as a hot-air balloon.[13]

'Experience and Poverty' is shot through with ambivalence. Towards the end, the exuberant apologia for modernity gives way again to a sober assessment that is more in line with Benjamin's deep-seated scepticism towards modernity. Prefiguring the Second World War, Benjamin writes:

> We have become impoverished. We have given up one portion of the human heritage after another, and have often left it at the pawnbroker's for a hundredth of its true value, in exchange for the small change of 'the contemporary.' The economic crisis is at the door, and behind it is the shadow of the approaching war.[14]

Modernity was at least a time that had *visions*. Glass, the real protagonist of Paul Scheerbart's visionary writings, was meant to be the medium of the future that would lift human culture to the next level. In his manifesto *Glass Architecture*, Scheerbart conjures the beauty of a world in which glass is the universal building material.

Glass architecture would transform the earth as if it were 'adorned with sparkling jewels and enamel'.[15] Then, 'all over the world it would be more splendid than in the gardens of the Arabian Nights'.[16] In a world of bright, colourful and seemingly hovering glass buildings, people would be happier. Scheerbart's visions concern beauty and human happiness, and they afford glass, the medium of the future, a particular aura. Real narratives about the future radiate an aura because the future is a *phenomenon of distance*.

Modernity is animated by a belief in progress, an atmosphere of departure, of clearing the tables and beginning anew, and by the spirit of revolution. *The Communist Manifesto* is also a narrative about the future; it resolutely turns away from the traditional order. The manifesto talks about 'the forcible overthrow of all existing social conditions'.[17] It is a *grand narrative* about the society to come. Modernity, to use a phrase coined by Bertolt Brecht, possesses a pronounced 'sense of beginning'. Having cleared the table, it plays on 'the great tabula rasa'.[18]

Unlike modernity, with its narratives of the future and progress – its longing for *another form of life* – late modernity does not have a revolutionary pathos of the new or of fresh beginnings. It lacks the spirit of departure. It is therefore declining into a mode of '*on and on*', of absent alternatives. It loses *narrative courage, the courage to create a world-changing narrative*. Storytelling is now mainly a matter of commercialism and consumption. As *storyselling*, it does not contain the power to bring about social change. This exhausted late modernity does not know the 'sense of beginning', the passion of 'beginning from the start'. We no longer *commit ourselves* to anything. We constantly *take the trouble* to do something. We succumb to *convenience* or to *likes*, which need no narrative. Late modernity knows no longing, no vision, no *distance*. It therefore *lacks aura*, that is, *lacks a future*.

Today's tsunami of information sharpens the narrative crisis by throwing us into a maelstrom of actuality. Information cuts up time. Time is reduced to the narrow track of what is momentarily relevant. It lacks temporal extension. The compulsion to actuality destabilizes our life. The past no longer has any effect in the present. The future is narrowed down; it becomes a stream of constant updates on what is currently relevant. We thus exist without a *history*, for a narrative is a *history*. We lose not only the capacity to have experiences, which are *condensed time*, but also the capacity to construct narratives of the future, which are based on a *temporal dispersal*. A life that trudges along from one present moment to the next, from one crisis to the next, from one problem to the next, slows to a mere survival. Living is more than just problem solving. Someone who merely solves problems does not have a future. It is only with *narrative* that a future opens up, for narrative gives us *hope*.

The Narrated Life

In *The Arcades Project*, Benjamin remarks:

> Happiness for us is thinkable only in the air that we have
> breathed, among the people who have lived with us.
> In other words, there vibrates in the idea of happiness
> ... the idea of salvation. ... Our life, it can be said,
> is a muscle strong enough to contract the whole of
> historical time. Or, to put it differently, the genuine
> conception of historical time rests entirely upon the
> image of redemption.[1]

Happiness is *not a momentary event*. It has a *long tail* that
reaches back into the past. Happiness feeds off all that has
been part of a life. It does not have a shiny appearance;
its appearance is an *afterglow*. We owe our happiness to
the *salvation of the past*. This salvation requires a *narrative*

tension in which the present *integrates* the past, thereby making the past a continuing influence, even resurrecting the past. In the state of happiness, salvation reverberates. When everything becomes part of a maelstrom of actuality, a storm of contingency, there can be no happiness for us.

Life, conceived as a muscle, would have to be enormously strong if men are, as Marcel Proust imagines, temporal beings who 'spend their lives perched upon living stilts which never cease to grow until sometimes they become taller than church steeples'.[2] The end of *In Search of Lost Time* is anything but triumphant:

> And I was terrified by the thought that the stilts beneath my own feet might already have reached that height; it seemed to me that quite soon now I might be too weak to maintain my hold upon a past which already went down so far.[3]

For Proust, the task of the narrator is to salvage the past:

> So if I were given long enough to accomplish my work, I should not fail, even if the effect were to make them resemble monsters, to describe men as occupying so considerable a place, compared with the restricted place which is reserved for them in space, a place on the contrary prolonged past measure ... in Time.[4]

In modernity, life atrophies. The decay of time is a threat to life. In his *In Search of Lost Time*, Proust is fighting against *temporal atrophy*, the *disappearance of time* as a kind of *muscular atrophy*. *Time Regained* appeared in 1927, the same year that saw the publication of Heidegger's *Being and Time*. Heidegger was also determined to use his writing to fight the *temporal atrophy* of modernity, the destabilization and fragmentation of life. To the fragmentation and withering of life in modernity he juxtaposes 'the whole of existence stretched along' in 'which Dasein [Heidegger's ontological term for human beings] as fate "incorporates" into its existence birth and death and their "between"'.[5] Human beings do not exist from one moment to the next. They are not momentary beings. Their existence comprises the whole temporal range that opens up between birth and death. In the absence of external orientation and a narrative anchoring in being, the energy to *contract* the time between birth and death into a living unity that encapsulates all events and occurrences must come from the self. The continuity of being is guaranteed by the continuity of the self. The 'constancy of the self' represents the central temporal axis that must protect us against the fragmentation of time.[6]

Heidegger claims that *Being and Time* is an ahistorical analysis of human existence, but it is in fact a reflection of the temporal crisis of modernity. Anxiety, which plays such a prominent role in *Being and Time*, is part of the pathology of modern man, who no longer has a firm footing in the world. Death itself is no longer integrated into a meaningful narrative of salvation. Rather, it is *my* death, and I have to deal with it by myself. As death puts an end to my self once and for all, Dasein – in the face of death – *contracts into itself*. From the constant presence of death comes the *pre-eminence of the self*. The *existential paroxysm* of a Dasein that is determined to realize its self generates the necessary tension, the muscular power that protects Dasein against the impending temporal atrophy and provides it with temporal continuity.

Heidegger's *'Being-one's-Self'* precedes narrative biographical context, which is constructed only later. Dasein assures itself of itself *before* it creates a coherent *worldly* story of itself. The self is not constructed out of worldly occurrences that were already connected with each other. 'Authentic historicality' is founded only by the pre-narrative 'whole of existence stretched along'. Against temporal atrophy, Heidegger seeks a *temporal framing of existence*, the 'whole of existence stretched along in this historicality in a way which is primordial and not lost, and which has no need of connectedness'.[7] This frame has to ensure that Dasein's *pre-narrative unity* does not disintegrate into 'momentary actualities of Experiences which come along successively and disappear'.[8] It pulls Dasein out of 'the endless multiplicity of possibilities which offer themselves as closest to one – those of comfortableness, shirking, and taking things lightly' – and anchors it in 'the simplicity of its fate [*Schicksals*]'.[9] Having a fate means *properly taking charge of one's self*. Someone who surrenders to the 'momentary actualities' has no fate, no 'authentic historicality'.

Digitalization intensifies the atrophy of time. Reality disintegrates into information that is relevant only briefly. Information lives on the allure of surprise. It thus fragments time. Our attention also becomes fragmented. Information does not permit any *lingering*. In the accelerated exchange of information, bits of information quickly replace each other. Snapchat is the embodiment of *instant digital communication*. This service is the purest expression of digital temporality. *Only the moment counts.* Snaps are a synonym for 'momentary actualities', and accordingly they disappear after a short while. Reality disintegrates into snaps. This removes the temporal anchors that stabilize us. 'Stories' on digital platforms such as Instagram or Facebook are not genuine stories. They have no *narrative duration.* Rather, they are just sequences of momentary impressions that do not tell us anything. They are in fact no more than bits of *visual information* that quickly disappear. *Nothing stays.* An Instagram advertisement says: '*Post* moments from your *everyday life* in your Stories. These are fun, casual, and only last 24 hours.' This temporal limitation creates a peculiar psychological effect. It evokes a feeling of fleetingness, which produces a subtle compulsion to communicate even more.

Selfies are *momentary photographs.* Their only concern is the moment. As a medium of remembrance, a selfie is fleeting visual information. Unlike an analogue photo, it is registered only briefly and then disappears for good. Selfies aim not at remembrance but at communication. Ultimately, they announce the end of the human being as someone with a fate and a history.

Phono sapiens surrenders to the 'momentary actualities of Experiences which come along successively and disappear'. The 'whole of existence stretched along' – which connects birth and death and gives a life its emphasis on the self – is alien to *Phono sapiens,* who does not exist historically. The phenomenon of the *funeral selfie* suggests this absence of death. Standing next to the coffin, people smile at their cameras. *Likes* can be elicited even from death. Apparently, *Phono sapiens* moves beyond *Homo sapiens,* who was in need of salvation.

With digital platforms such as Twitter, Facebook, Instagram, TikTok and Snapchat, we approach the degree zero of narration. They are media of information, not narration. They work in an additive rather than narrative fashion. The strings of information do not condense into a narrative. To the question 'How do I add or edit a life event on my Facebook profile?' the answer is: 'Scroll down to posts and tap *life event.*' Life events are mere bits of information. They are not woven into an extended narrative but simply added up into a *syndetic* arrangement. There is no *narrative synthesis* of events. On digital platforms, lived moments cannot be digested and condensed in a reflexive and narrative manner – and in fact this is intentional. Digital platforms' technical dispositif rules out time-intensive narrative practices.

Human memory is selective. This is how it differs from a database. It is narrative, whereas digital memories are additive and cumulative. A narrative depends on a selection and connection of events. It proceeds in a selective fashion. The narrative path is narrow. It comprises only selected events. The narrated or remembered life is necessarily *incomplete*. Digital platforms, by contrast, seek to create a *complete record of a life. The less narration there is, the more data and information there are.* For digital platforms, data are more valuable than narratives. They do not want *narrative reflection.* When digital platforms permit narrative formats, these must be designed so as to be compatible with databases. They need to produce as many data as possible. The narrative formats therefore necessarily have an additive form. 'Stories' are designed to be bearers of information; narrative, in the genuine

21

sense, disappears. The dispositif of digital platforms is: the *total record of a life*. The aim is to translate a life into a dataset. The more data there are about a person, the better that person can be surveilled, controlled and economically exploited. *Phono sapiens* believe they are merely playing, but they are in fact being utterly exploited and controlled. The smartphone seems to be a playground, but it is a *digital panopticon*.

Creating an autobiographical narrative requires one to reflect on one's life – the conscious work of remembrance. Data and information, by contrast, are generated in a way that *bypasses consciousness*. They represent our activities immediately, without any reflective filtering. *If data are produced in a less conscious way, they are accordingly more useful.* Such data provide access to those regions that lie outside of consciousness. They allow digital platforms to screen a person and to control their behaviour at a pre-reflexive level.

Walter Benjamin suggested that, just as psychoanalysis discovers the 'instinctual unconscious', the technical possibilities of the camera, such as slow motion, time lapses and close-ups, allow us to discover an 'optical unconscious'.[10] In a similar way, data mining acts as a digital magnifying glass that discloses an unconscious space behind the conscious one. We may call this space the *digital unconscious*. It allows artificial intelligence to access our unconscious desires and inclinations. This puts *data-driven psychopolitics* in a position to control our behaviour at a pre-reflexive level.[11]

In the case of so-called 'self-tracking', counting completely supplants narration. All that self-tracking generates are data. The motto of the Quantified Self movement is 'Self-Knowledge through Numbers'. Its adherents try to gain self-knowledge not through narration, remembrance and reflection, but by way of counting and numbers. To this end, the body is fitted with various sensors that automatically generate data on heart rate, blood pressure, body temperature, movement and sleep patterns. Mental states and moods are continuously monitored. A detailed log of all everyday activities is kept. Even the day one notices one's first grey hair is recorded. Nothing must escape the total record of a life. In all this, *nothing is narrated*. Everything is measured. Sensors and apps provide data automatically, *without any linguistic representation or narrative reflection*. The collected data are then summarized in visually appealing graphics and diagrams. These, however, do not say anything about who I am. *The self is not a quantity but a quality*. 'Self-Knowledge through Numbers' is an illusion. Self-knowledge can be generated only through narration. *I must narrate myself*. But numbers do not narrate anything. The expression 'numerical narratives' is an oxymoron. A life cannot be captured through quantifiable events.

The third episode of the first series of *Black Mirror* is called *The Entire History of You*. It depicts a transparent society in which everyone wears an implant behind the ear that records everything the wearer sees and experiences. Everything that was seen or perceived can be replayed, either directly to the wearer or on an external screen. At airport security checks, for instance, the officer asks you to replay the events of a certain time period. Nothing is secret any more. It is impossible for criminals to hide their crimes. People are, so to speak, captured in their own memories. Strictly speaking, when everything that is experienced can be repeated, remembrance is impossible.

Remembrance is not a mechanical repetition of an earlier experience but a narrative that must be recounted again and again. Memories necessarily have gaps. They presuppose *closeness* and *distance*. When all experience is *present and distanceless*, that is, when it is *available*, remembrance is impossible. The gapless repetition of past experience is not a narrative but a *report* or *record*. To be able to narrate or remember, one must *be able to forget* or *leave out* a great deal. The transparency society spells the end of narrative and remembrance. There is no such thing as a transparent narrative. *Only information and data are transparent.* In the final scene of *The Entire History of You*, the protagonist takes a razor blade to himself, and cuts out the implant.

Bare Life

The protagonist of Sartre's *Nausea*, Roquentin, is one day overcome by an unbearable nausea:

> Then the Nausea seized me, I dropped to a seat, I no longer knew where I was; I saw the colours spin slowly around me, I wanted to vomit. And since that time, the Nausea has not left me, it holds me.[1]

To Roquentin, the nausea appears to be a property of things. He picks up a pebble and feels 'a sort of nausea in the hands'.[2] The world *is* nausea: 'The Nausea is not inside me: I feel it *out there* in the wall, in the suspenders, everywhere around me. It makes itself one with the café, I am the one who is within *it*.'[3]

Gradually, Roquentin comes to realize that it is the pure presence of the things, sheer facticity, the contingency of the world that triggers the nausea. Under his gaze, the meaningful relations that negate the accidental and insignificant nature of things disintegrate. The world appears to him to be naked. It is divested of all meaning. His own existence also seems meaningless:

> I had appeared by chance, I existed like a stone, a plant, or microbe. My life proceeded at random and in every direction. Sometimes it gave me vague signals; at other times I felt nothing more than a meaningless buzzing.[4]

The meaningless buzzing is unbearable. There is no *music*, no *tone*. Everywhere there is an unbearable emptiness in which Roquentin might suffocate. The world does not *mean* anything to him. Nor does he *understand* it. There are no purposes; there is no 'in-order-to' to which he could subject things. It is precisely the purpose, the use, the *servility* of things that keeps them at a distance. Now, they impose their naked presence on Roquentin. They develop an independence:

> Objects should not touch because they are not alive. You use them, put them back in place, you live among them: they are useful, nothing more. But they touch me, it is unbearable. I am afraid of being in contact with them as though they were living beasts.[5]

One day, Roquentin is struck by the idea that narrating has the power to make the world appear meaningful:

> This is what I thought: for the most banal event to become an adventure, you must (and this is enough)

begin to recount it. This is what fools people: a man is always a teller of tales, he lives surrounded by his stories and the stories of others, he sees everything that happens to him through them; and he tries to live his own life as if he were telling a story.

But you have to choose: live or tell.[6]

Only with narration is life elevated above its sheer facticity, above its nakedness. Narrating means to make time's passing meaningful, to give it a *beginning* and an *end*. Without narration, life is purely additive:

Nothing happens when you live. The scenery changes, people come in and go out, that's all. There are no beginnings. Days are tacked on to days without rhyme or reason, as interminable, monotonous addition. From time to time you make a semi-total: you say: I have been travelling for three years, I've been in Bouville for three years. Neither is there any end ... the procession starts again, you begin to add up hours and days: Monday, Tuesday, Wednesday. April, May, June. 1924, 1925, 1926.[7]

Modernity's existential crisis – a crisis of narration – is caused by the splitting of *life* and *narrative*, as summed up in the choice 'live or tell'. Life, it seems, can no longer be narrated. In pre-modern times, life was anchored in narratives. In time as narration, there is not only Monday, Tuesday, Wednesday ... but also Easter, Whitsun, Christmas – narrative points of reference. Even the days of the week have narrative meaning: Wednesday is the day of Woden, Thursday the day of Thor and so on.

Roquentin tries to overcome the unbearable facticity of being, bare life, by way of narrative. At the end of the book, he resolves to give up his profession as a historian and become a writer. Writing, he believes, will allow him to *salvage the past*:

> A book. Naturally, at first it would only be a troublesome, tiring work, it wouldn't stop me from existing or feeling that I exist. But a time would come when the book would be written, when it would be behind me, and I think that a little of its clarity might fall over my past. Then, perhaps, I could remember my life without repugnance.[8]

The *perception of the world in narrative form* is blissful. Everything enters into a well-formed order. The narrative 'and' feeds off the imagination; it unites things and events, even trifling, insignificant or incidental things, into a story. Without this bringing together, which overcomes *sheer facticity*, things and events would have nothing to do with each other. But through it, the world appears *rhythmically structured*. Things and events are not isolated; they are elements belonging to a narrative. In his 'Essay on the Jukebox', Peter Handke writes:

> And now, as he aimlessly checked out the trails in the savanna, suddenly an entirely new rhythm sprang up in him, not an alternating, sporadic one, but a single, steady one, and, above all, one that, instead of circling and flirting around, went straight and with complete seriousness in medias res: the rhythm of narrative. At first he experienced everything he encountered as he

went along as narrative songs . . .: 'Thistles had blown into the wire fence. An older man with a plastic bag bent down for a mushroom. A dog hopped by on three legs and made one think of a deer . . . In the train from Zaragoza the lights were already lit, and a handful of people sat in the carriages . . .'[9]

Elsewhere, Handke sees narrative perception that goes beyond sheer facticity as an existential strategy for transforming frightening being-in-the-world into familiar being-at-home – a way of imposing connections on the isolated and unconnected. The narrative, experienced as something divine, reveals itself to be an existential compulsion:

> This was no longer the compelling, warming power of imagery carrying him along, but clearly a cold compulsion, ascending from his heart to his head, a senseless repeated hurling of himself against a gate long since closed, and he wondered whether narration, which had first seemed divine, hadn't been a snare and a delusion – an expression of his fear in the face of all the isolated, unconnected phenomena?[10]

Life in late modernity is utterly naked. It lacks *narrative imagination*. Pieces of information cannot be tied together into a narrative. Things thus break free. The coherence from which events derive their meaning gives way to a meaningless side-by-side and one-after-the-other. There is no narrative horizon that lifts us above mere life. Life that must be kept 'healthy' and 'optimized' is mere survival. The manic pursuit of health and the optimization of life can occur only in a naked and meaningless world. Optimization is concerned only with functioning and efficiency. A narrative, by contrast, cannot be optimized, because it has intrinsic value.

In digital late modernity, we conceal the nakedness – the absence of meaning in our lives – by constantly posting, liking and sharing. The noise of communication and information is supposed to ensure that life's terrifying vacuity remains hidden. Today's crisis is expressed not in the choice 'live *or* tell' but in the choice 'live *or* post'. The reason that people compulsively take selfies is not narcissism. Rather, it is *inner emptiness*. There is no meaning to stabilize the ego. Faced with its inner emptiness, the ego constantly *produces itself*. Selfies reproduce the *self in its empty form*.

In the information and transparency society, nakedness intensifies and becomes obscenity. However, this is not the charged obscenity of the repressed, prohibited or secret, but the empty obscenity of transparency, information and communication: 'It is the obscenity of what no longer harbours any secret, what can be dissolved without remainder into information and communication.'[11] Information as such is pornographic, because it has *no cover*. Eloquent, narrating is only the *cover*, the *veil* that weaves itself around the things. Covering and veiling are essential to narrative. Pornography does not tell anything. It gets right *down to it*, whereas the *eroticism of narrative* indulges in *incidental details*.

The Disenchantment of the World

The children's author Paul Maar tells the story of a boy who cannot tell stories.[1] When his little sister, Susanne, is struggling to fall asleep, tossing and turning in her bed, she asks Konrad to tell her a story. He declines in a huff. Konrad's parents, by contrast, love telling stories. They are almost addicted to it, and they argue over who will go first. They therefore decide to keep a list, so that everyone gets a go. When Roland, the father, has told a story, the mother puts an 'R' on the list. When Olivia, the mother, tells a story, the father enters a large 'O'. Every now and again, a small 'S' finds its way on to the list in between all the 'Rs' and 'Os' – Susanne, too, is beginning to enjoy telling stories. The family forms a small story-telling community. Konrad is the exception.

The family is particularly in the mood for stories during breakfast at the weekend. Narrating requires leisure.

31

Under conditions of accelerated communication, we do not have the time, or even the patience, to tell stories. We merely exchange information. Under more leisurely conditions, anything can trigger a narrative. The father, for instance, asks the mother: 'Olivia, could you pass the jam please?' As soon as he grasps the jam jar, he gazes dreamily, and *narrates*:

> This reminds me of my grandfather. One day, I might have been eight or nine, grandpa asked for strawberry jam over lunch. Lunch, mind you! At first we thought we had misunderstood him, because we were having a roast with baked potatoes, as we always did on 2 September . . .

'This reminds me of . . .' and 'one day' are the ways in which the father introduces his narrations. Narration and remembrance cause each other. Someone who lives completely in the moment cannot narrate anything.

The mismatch between the roast and strawberry jam creates the narrative tension. It invokes the whole story of someone's life, the drama or tragedy of a person's biography. The profound inwardness betrayed by the father's dreamlike gaze nourishes the remembrance as narration. Post-narrative time is a time without inwardness. Information turns everything towards the outside. Instead of the *inwardness of a narrator*, we have the *alertness of an information hunter*.

The memory prompted by the strawberry jam is reminiscent of Proust's *mémoire involontaire*. In a hotel room in the seaside town of Balbec, Proust bends down to untie his shoelaces, and is suddenly confronted with an image of his late grandmother. The painful memory of his beloved grandmother brings tears to his eyes, but it also gives him a moment of happiness. In a *mémoire involontaire*, two separate moments in time combine into one *fragrant crystal of time*. The torturous contingency of time is thereby overcome, and this produces happiness. By establishing strong connections between events, a narrative overcomes the emptiness and fleetingness of time. *Narrative time does not pass.* This is why the loss of our narrative capacities intensifies the experience of contingency. This loss means we are subject to transience and contingency. The memory of the grandmother's face is also experienced as her *true* image. We recognize the *truth* only in hindsight. Truth has its place in *remembrance as narration*.

Time is becoming increasingly atomized. Narrating a story, by contrast, consists in establishing connections. Whoever narrates in the Proustian sense delves into life and inwardly weaves new threads between events. In this way, a narrator forms a dense network of relations in which nothing remains isolated. Everything appears to be meaningful. It is through narrative that we escape the contingency of life.

Konrad cannot narrate because his world consists exclusively of facts. Instead of telling stories, he enumerates these facts. When his mother asks him about yesterday, he replies: 'Yesterday, I was in school. First, we had maths, then German, then biology, and then two hours of sports. Then I went home and did my homework. Then, I spent some time at the computer, and later I went to bed.' His life is determined by external events. He lacks the inwardness that would allow him to internalize events and to weave and condense them into a story.

His little sister wants to help him. She suggests: 'I always begin by saying: there once was a mouse.' Konrad immediately interrupts her: 'Shrew, house mouse, or vole?' Then he continues: 'Mice belong to the genus rodents. There are two groups. Genuine mice and voles.' Konrad's world is fully disenchanted. It disintegrates into facts and loses narrative tension. The world that can be explained cannot be narrated.

Eventually, Konrad's mother and father realize that he cannot narrate. They decide to send him to Ms Leishure, who taught them how to tell stories. One rainy day, Konrad goes to see Ms Leishure. At her door, he is welcomed by a friendly old lady with white hair and thick, still dark eyebrows: 'I understand that your parents have sent you to me so that you can learn how to tell stories.' From the outside, the house appears to be very small, but inside there is a seemingly endless corridor. Ms Leishure puts a parcel in Konrad's hands and, pointing to a small staircase, asks him to take it upstairs to her sister. Konrad ascends the stairs, which seem to go on forever. Astonished, he asks: 'How is this possible? I saw the house from the outside, and it had only one floor. We must be on the seventh by now.' Konrad notices that he is all alone. Suddenly, in the wall next to him a low door opens. A hoarse voice calls out: 'Ah, there you arse at last. Now home on and come bin!' Everything seems enchanted. Language itself is a strange riddle; it has something magical about it, as if it is under a spell. Konrad pokes his head through the door. In the darkness, he is able to make out an owlish figure. Frightened, he asks: 'Who . . . who are you?' 'Don't be so purrious. Do you want to let me wait foreven?' the owlish creature retorts. Konrad stoops to go through the door. 'Soon you'll blow downhill! Have a lice trip!' the voice chuckles. At that very moment, Konrad notices that the dark room has no floor. He falls downwards through a tube at breakneck pace. He tries in vain to find something to hold on to, all the time feeling as though he has been swallowed by some enormous animal. The tube eventually spits him out at Ms Leishure's feet. 'What did you do with the parcel?' she asks angrily. 'I must have lost it along the way', Konrad answers. Ms Leishure puts her hand in a pocket of her dark dress and pulls out another parcel. Konrad could have sworn that it was the very same one she gave him earlier. 'Here', Ms Leishure says brusquely. 'Please deliver this to my brother downstairs.' 'In the basement?' Konrad asks. 'Nonsense', says Ms Leishure. 'You'll find him on the ground floor. We are up on the seventh floor, as you know! Now go!' Konrad cautiously descends the small staircase, which again seems to go on forever. After a hundred steps, Konrad reaches a dark corridor. 'Hello', he hesitantly calls out. No one answers. Konrad tries 'Hello, Mr Leishure! Can you hear me?' A door next to Konrad opens, and a coarse voice says: 'Of course, I swear you. I'm not deaf! Quick, come wine!' In the dark room there is a seated figure who looks like a beaver and smokes a cigar. The beaver creature asks: 'What are you baiting for? Come on nine!' Konrad slowly enters the room. Again he falls into the dark bowels of the house, and again they spit him out at Ms Leishure's feet. She draws on a thin cigar and says: 'Let me guess? You failed to deliver the parcel again.' Konrad musters his courage to say: 'No. But anyway, I am not here to deliver parcels but to learn how to tell stories.' 'How can I teach a boy who cannot even carry a parcel upstairs how to tell a story! You'd better go home – you are a hopeless case', Ms Leishure says confidently. She opens a door in the wall next to him: 'Have a safe journey dome and all the west', she says, pushing him out. Again Konrad slides down through the endless twists and turns of the house. This time, however, he ends up not at Ms Leishure's feet but directly in front of his house. His parents and sister are still having breakfast when Konrad comes rushing into the house, announcing excitedly: 'I have to tell you something. You will never believe what happened to me . . .'. For Konrad, the world is now no longer intelligible. It consists not of objective facts but of events that resist explanation, and for that very reason require narration. His narrative turn makes Konrad a member of the small narrative community. His mother and father smile at each other. 'There you go!' his mother says. She puts a big 'K' on the list.

Paul Maar's story reads like a subtle social critique. It seems to lament the fact that we have unlearned how to tell stories. And this loss of our narrative capacity is attributed to the disenchantment of the world. This disenchantment can be reduced to the formula: things *are*, but they are *mute*. The magic evaporates from them. The pure facticity of existence makes narrative impossible. Facticity and narration are mutually exclusive.

The disenchantment of the world means first and foremost that our relationship to the world is reduced to causality. But causality is only *one* kind of relationship. The hegemony of causality leads to a poverty in world and experience. A magical world is one in which things enter into relations with each other that are not ruled by causal connections – relations in which things exchange intimacies. Causality is a mechanical and external relation. Magical and poetic relationships to the world rest on a deep *sympathy* that connects humans and things. In *The Disciples at Saïs*, Novalis says:

> Does not the rock become an individual 'thou' when I address it? And what else am I than the river when I gaze with melancholy in its waves, and my thoughts are lost in its course? . . . Whether any one has yet understood the stones or the stars I know not, but such a one must certainly have been a gifted being.[2]

For Walter Benjamin, children are the last inhabitants of a magical world. For them, nothing merely *exists*. Everything is *eloquent* and *meaningful*. A *magical intimacy* connects them with the world. In play, they transform themselves into things and in this way come into close contact with them:

> Standing behind the doorway curtain, the child himself becomes something floating and white, a ghost. The dining table under which he is crouching turns him into the wooden idol in a temple whose four pillars are the carved legs. And behind a door, he himself *is* the door – wears it as his heavy mask, and like a shaman will bewitch all those who unsuspectingly enter. . . . the apartment is the arsenal of his masks. Yet once each year – in mysterious places, in their empty eye sockets, in their fixed mouths – presents lie. Magical experience becomes science. As its engineer, the child disenchants

the gloomy parental apartment and looks for Easter eggs.[3]

Today, children have become profane, digital beings. The magical experience of the world has withered. Children hunt for information, their *digital Easter eggs*.

The disenchantment of the world is expressed in de-auratization. The aura is the radiance that raises the world above its mere facticity, the mysterious veil around things. The aura has a narrative core. Benjamin points out that the narrative memory images of *mémoire involontaire* possess an aura, whereas photographic images do not: 'If the distinctive feature of the images arising from *mémoire involontaire* is seen in their aura, then photography is decisively implicated in the phenomenon of a "decline of the aura".'[4]

Photographs are distinguished from memory images by their lack of narrative inwardness. Photographs represent what is there without internalizing it. They do not mean anything. Memory as narration, by contrast, does not represent a spatiotemporal continuum. Rather, it is based on a *narrative selection*. Unlike photography, memory is decidedly arbitrary and incomplete. It expands or contracts temporal distances. It leaves out years or decades.[5] Narrativity is opposed to logical facticity.

Following a suggestion in Proust, Benjamin believes that things retain within themselves the gaze that looked on them.[6] They themselves thus become gaze-like. The gaze helps to weave the auratic veil that surrounds things. Aura is the 'distance of the gaze that is awakened in what is looked at'.[7] When looked at intently, things return our gaze:

The person we look at, or who feels he is being looked at, looks at us in turn. To experience the aura of an object we look at means to invest it with the ability to look back at us. This ability corresponds to the data of *mémoire involontaire*.[8]

When things lose their aura, they lose their magic – they neither look at us nor speak to us. They are no longer a 'thou' but a mute 'it'. We no longer *exchange gazes* with the world.

When they are submerged in the fluid medium of *mémoire involontaire*, things become fragrant vessels in which what was seen and felt is condensed in narrative fashion. Names, too, take on an aura and *narrate*: 'A name read long ago in a book contains within its syllables the strong wind and brilliant sunshine that prevailed while we were reading it.'[9] Words, too, can radiate an aura. Benjamin quotes Karl Kraus: 'The closer one looks at a word, the greater the distance from which it looks back.'[10]

Today, we primarily perceive the world with a view to getting information. Information has neither distance nor expanse. It cannot hold rough winds or dazzling sunshine. It lacks auratic space. Information therefore de-auratizes and disenchants the world. When language decays into information, it loses its aura. Information is the endpoint of atrophied language.

Memory is a narrative practice that connects events in novel combinations and creates a network of relations. The tsunami of information destroys narrative inwardness. De-narrativized memories resemble 'junk-shops – great dumps of images of all kinds and origins, used and shop-soiled symbols, piled up any old how'.[11] The things in a junk shop are a chaotic, disorderly heap. *The heap is the counter-figure of narrative.* Events coalesce into a *story* only when they are *stratified* in a particular way. Heaps of data or information are storyless. They are not narrative but cumulative.

The story is the counter-figure of information insofar as it has a beginning and an end. It is characterized by closure. It is a *concluding form*:

> There is an essential – as I see it – distinction between stories, on the one hand, which have as their goal, an end, completeness, closure, and, on the other hand, information, which is always, by definition, partial, incomplete, fragmentary.[12]

A completely unbounded world lacks enchantment and magic. Enchantment depends on boundaries, transitions and thresholds. Susan Sontag writes:

> For there to be completeness, unity, coherence, there must be borders. Everything is relevant in the journey we take within those borders. One could describe the story's end as a point of magical convergence for the shifting preparatory views: a fixed position from which the reader sees how initially disparate things finally belong together.[13]

Narrative is a play of light and shadow, of the visible and invisible, of nearness and distance. *Transparency* destroys this dialectical tension, which forms the basis of every narrative. The digital disenchantment of the world goes far beyond the disenchantment that Max Weber attributed to scientific rationalization. *Today's disenchantment is the result of the informatization of the world. Transparency is the new formula of disenchantment.* Transparency disenchants the world by dissolving it into data and information.

In an interview, Paul Virilio mentions a science-fiction short story about the invention of a tiny camera. It is so small and light that it can be transported by a snowflake. Extraordinary numbers of these cameras are mixed into artificial snow and then dropped from aeroplanes. People think it is snowing, but in fact the world is being contaminated with cameras. The world becomes fully transparent. Nothing remains hidden. There are no more blind spots. Asked what we will dream of when everything becomes visible, Virilio answers: 'We'll dream of being blind.'[14] There is no such thing as a *transparent narrative.* Every narrative needs secrets and enchantment. Only our dreams of blindness would save us from the hell of transparency, would return to us the capacity to narrate.

Gershom Scholem concludes one of his books on Jewish mysticism with a Hasidic tale:

When the Baal Shem had a difficult task before him, he would go to a certain place in the woods, light a fire and meditate in prayer – and what he had set out to perform was done. When a generation later the 'Maggid' of Meseritz was faced with the same task he would go to the same place in the woods and say: We can no longer light the fire, but we can still speak the prayers – and what he wanted done became reality. Again a generation later Rabbi Moshe Leib of Sassov had to perform this task. And he too went into the woods and said: We can no longer light a fire, nor do we know the

41

secret meditations belonging to the prayer, but we do know the place in the woods to which it all belongs – and that must be sufficient; and sufficient it was. But when another generation had passed and Rabbi Israel of Rishin was called upon to perform the task, he sat down on his golden chair in his castle and said: We cannot light the fire, we cannot speak the prayers, we do not know the place, but we can tell the story of how it was done. And, the story-teller adds, the story which he told had the same effect as the actions of the other three.[15]

Theodor W. Adorno quotes this Hasidic tale in full in his 'Gruß an Gershom Scholem: Zum 70. Geburtstag' [Greetings to Gershom Scholem on his seventieth birthday].[16] He interprets the story as a metaphor for the advance of secularization in modernity. The world becomes increasingly disenchanted. The mythical fire has long since burnt itself out. We no longer know how to say prayers. We are not able to engage in secret meditation. The mythical place in the woods has also been forgotten. Today, we must add to this list: we are losing the *capacity to tell the story* through which we can invoke this mythical past.

From Shocks to Likes

In his essay 'On Some Motifs in Baudelaire', Walter Benjamin quotes from a short prose piece by Baudelaire, 'Perte d'auréole' [Loss of a Halo]. It tells the story of a poet who loses his halo while crossing a boulevard:

> A short while ago I was hurrying across the boulevard, and amid that churning chaos in which death comes galloping at you from all sides at once I must have made an awkward movement, for the halo slipped off my head and fell into the mire of the macadam.[1]

Benjamin interprets the story as an allegory of the disintegration of the aura in modernity. Baudelaire 'named the price for which the sensation of modernity could be had: the disintegration of the aura in immediate shock experience [*Chockerlebnis*]'.[2] Reality impacts on the observer via the shock. Its representation moves from the canvas to the projection screen. A painting invites the observer to linger in front of it in contemplation and to enter into free association. *The observers rest in themselves.* The spectator at the movies, by contrast, resembles the pedestrian in the middle of chaotic traffic where death approaches on all sides: 'Film is the art form corresponding to the increased threat to life that faces people today.'[3]

According to Freud, the main function of consciousness is to protect us against stimuli. Consciousness tries to assign the received stimulus a place within itself, at the expense of the integrity of the conscious material. Benjamin quotes Freud:

> For a living organism, protection against stimuli is almost more important than the reception of stimuli. The protective shield is equipped with its own store of energy and must above all strive to preserve the special forms of conversion of energy operating in it against the effects of the excessive energies at work in the external world-effects that tend toward an equalization of potential and hence toward destruction.

'The threat posed by these energies', Benjamin says, 'is the threat of shocks. The more readily consciousness registers these shocks, the less likely they are to have a traumatic effect.'[4] Consciousness prevents stimuli from reaching the deeper layers of the psyche. When consciousness's protection against stimuli fails, we suffer a traumatic shock. Dreaming and remembering are delayed ways of coming to terms with such shocks. They take the time that was originally lacking and deal with the stimuli in hindsight. If consciousness succeeds in parrying the shock, the impact of the occurrence is weakened, and it becomes an event. In the modern age, the shock aspect of individual impressions has become so intensified that our consciousness is forced to be permanently active as a shield against stimuli. The more it succeeds in this endeavour, the less the stimuli become part of our *experience*. Experiences [*Erfahrungen*] are replaced with events [*Erlebnisse*], that is, with attenuated shocks. The eye of the modern city dweller is overburdened with protective tasks. It unlearns contemplative lingering: 'In the protective eye, there is no daydreaming surrender to distance and to faraway things.'[5]

Benjamin turns the experience of shocks into Baudelaire's poetic principle. Baudelaire

> speaks of a duel in which the artist, just before being beaten, screams in fright. This duel is the creative process itself. Thus, Baudelaire placed shock experience [*Chockerfahrung*] at the very center of his art. . . . Since Baudelaire was himself vulnerable to being frightened, it was not unusual for him to evoke fright. Valles tells us about his eccentric grimaces . . . Gautier speaks of the italicizing Baudelaire indulged in when reciting poetry; Nadar describes his jerky gait.

According to Benjamin, Baudelaire was one of those 'traumatophile types'. He 'made it his business to parry the shocks . . . with his spiritual and physical self'.[6] He '*stabs away*' with his pencil.

More than 100 years have passed since Benjamin published his essay on Baudelaire. The screens on which movies played have been replaced by digital screens that we look at almost constantly. Etymologically, a screen [*Schirm*] is a protective barrier. A screen *bans* reality, which becomes an image, thus screening us off from it. We perceive reality almost exclusively via digital screens. Reality has become merely a section of the screen. On a smartphone screen, reality is so attenuated that it can no longer create any shock experiences. *Shocks give way to likes.*

Because it removes reality's *gaze*, the smartphone is a most efficient tool for screening us off from reality. Reality's gaze is the gaze through which the *other* addresses us. Reality as *something facing us* disappears entirely behind the touchscreen. Deprived of its otherness, the other becomes consumable. According to Lacan, a picture still possesses a gaze that looks at me, captures me, enchants and fascinates me, that puts me under its spell and takes hold of my eyes: 'certainly, in the picture, something of the gaze is always manifested'.[7] Lacan distinguishes between the gaze and the eyes. The eyes construct an imaginary mirror image that *the gaze crosses out*.

A countenance demands distance. It is a *thou* and not an available *it*. It is possible to put one's finger on the picture of a person, or even erase it, only because it has already lost its gaze – the countenance. Lacan would say that the picture on the touchscreen is *without gaze*, that it serves only to please my eyes and satisfy my needs. In this, the touchscreen differs from the picture as a *screen (écran)* behind which the gaze still *remains visible*. Because the digital screen completely seals us off from reality, nothing *remains visible* behind it. The digital screen is *flat*.

46

Every theory of the picture reflects the society to which it belongs. During Lacan's time, the world was still experienced as having a gaze. In Heidegger, we also find formulations that sound odd today. In 'The Origin of the Work of Art' (1935–6), he writes about 'equipment' [*Zeug*], such as an axe, jug or shoes: 'Serviceability is the basic trait from out of which these kinds of beings look at us – that is, flash at us and thereby presence and so be the beings they are.'[8] In fact, it is serviceability that makes the being-present of beings disappear, because we perceive equipment only with regard to its purpose. Heidegger's 'equipment' still retains the dimension of a gaze. It is *something facing us*, looking at us.

The disappearance of the gaze accompanies the narcissization of perception. Narcissism removes the gaze, that is, the other, and puts an imaginary mirror image in its place. Smartphones accelerate the expulsion of the other. They are digital mirrors that bring about a post-infantile return of the mirror stage. The use of smartphones means that we remain in a mirror stage that upholds an imaginary ego. The digital subjects Lacan's triad of the real, the imaginary and the symbolic to a radical reconstruction. It dismantles the real and replaces the symbolic, which embodies shared values and norms, with the imaginary. Ultimately, the digital leads to the erosion of community.

In the age of Netflix, no one speaks of having shock experiences in connection with films. A Netflix series is nothing like a piece of art that corresponds to a pronounced danger to life and limb. Rather, it typically leads to *binge watching*. Viewers are fattened like consumer cattle. *Binge watching* is a paradigm for the general mode of perception in digital late modernity.

The *transformation from shocks to likes* can also be derived from a change in our psychic apparatus. It may be true that the increasing sensory overload in modernity is experienced as a shock. But over time, the psychic apparatus gets used to the increased stimuli, and perception becomes accordingly dulled. The cortex of the brain where our defences against stimuli are located becomes calloused, so to speak. The outermost layer of consciousness hardens and becomes 'to some degree inorganic'.[9]

The type of artist represented by Baudelaire, someone who inadvertently causes fright, would today seem not only antiquated but almost grotesque. The artist who typifies our age is Jeff Koons. He appears *smart*. His works reflect the smooth consumer world that is the opposite of the world of shocks. All Koons wants from his audience is a simple 'Wow!' His art is intentionally relaxed and disarming. What he wants above all is *to be liked*. His motto is: 'embrace the viewer'. There is nothing in his art that is intended to frighten or rattle the viewer. His art is located beyond the world of shocks. Its aim, Koons says, is 'communication'. He could also have said: *the watchword of my art is the like*.

Theory as Narrative

In his essay 'The End of Theory', Chris Anderson, editor-in-chief of *Wired*, claims that incredibly large amounts of data make theories superfluous: 'Today companies like Google, which have grown up in an era of massively abundant data, don't have to settle for wrong models. Indeed, they don't have to settle for models at all.'[1] Human behaviour, he writes, can be precisely predicted and controlled with the help of data-driven psychology or sociology. The place of theory is taken by direct correlations between data:

> Out with every theory of human behavior, from linguistics to sociology. Forget taxonomy, ontology, and psychology. Who knows why people do what they do? The point is they do it, and we can track and measure it with unprecedented fidelity. With enough data, the numbers speak for themselves.

But big data does not explain anything. Big data merely discloses *correlations* between things. Correlations are the most primitive form of knowledge. They do not allow us to understand anything. Big data cannot explain *why* things are correlated in the way they are. It does not establish causal or conceptual connections. The question '*why?*' is replaced with a *non-conceptual 'this-is-how-it-is'*.

As a narrative, theory designs an order of things, setting them in relation to each other. Theory thereby explains *why* they behave the way they do. It develops *conceptual contexts* that make things intelligible. Unlike big data, theory offers us the highest form of knowledge: *comprehension*. Theory is a *form of closure* that *takes hold of things* and thereby makes them graspable. Big data, by contrast, is completely *open*. Theory, as a form of closure, *comprises* things *within* a conceptual framework and thus makes them *graspable*. The end of theory ultimately means the end of *concept as spirit* [*Begriff als Geist*]. Artificial intelligence can do without the conceptual. *Intelligence is not spirit*. Only spirit is capable of a reordering of things, of creating a new narrative. Intelligence computes and counts. *Spirit, however, recounts*. Data-driven human sciences [*Geisteswissenschaften*] are not sciences of *spirit* but data science. *Data drive out spirit*. Data-knowledge marks the *degree zero of spirit*. In a world saturated with data and information, our narrative capacity withers. Fewer theories are therefore formulated – no one wants to take the *risk* of putting forward a theory.

That a theory is actually a narrative is clear from the work of Sigmund Freud. His psychoanalysis is a narrative that offers a model for explaining the workings of our psychic apparatus. He subjects his patients' stories to his psychoanalytic narrative, which allows us to understand a particular kind of behaviour or a particular symptom. The cure is said to be successful when the patient accepts the narrative that he offers them. The case histories, as told by his patients, and his psychoanalytic narrative interact with each other. The psychoanalytic narrative is continually retold in light of the material Freud is trying to interpret. The stories told by the patients are meant to be fully absorbed by Freud's narrative. In this process, Freud becomes the hero of his own narrative:

> As a re-teller of that which has been told to him in a distorted way, he proves to be more than simply the person who brings all inconsistent information into focus, weighing and ordering it. He is never in danger of being impacted by the story, as he never loses his interpretive distance from any potential repercussions. We might even claim that the more the material to be interpreted threatens to escape his grasp, the more stubbornly he insists on his explanatory psychoanalytic formulas. And in doing so, he reveals himself as the hidden hero of his own analytic narratives.[2]

Plato's dialogues are an early illustration of the fact that philosophy is also a narrative. Plato may often, in the name of truth, be critical of myth as narrative, but paradoxically he frequently makes use of mythical stories himself. In some of his dialogues they play a central role. In *Phaedo*, for instance, Plato tells the story of the soul's fate after death, just as Dante does in his *Divine Comedy*. Sinners are condemned to eternal torture and 'hurled into Tartarus'.[3] Only the virtuous go to heaven after their death. Plato concludes his elaborations on the fate of the soul after death by saying:

> No sensible man would insist that these things are as I have described them, but I think it is fitting for a man to risk the belief – for the risk is a noble one – that this, or something like this, is true about our souls and their dwelling places, since the soul is evidently immortal, and a man should repeat this to himself as if it were an incantation, which is why I have been prolonging my tale [*mythos*].[4]

Philosophy, in the form of 'poetry' (*mythos*), takes a *risk*, a *noble risk*. It narrates – even *risks to suggest* – *a new form of life and being*. Descartes's *ego cogito, ergo sum* introduces a new order of things that represents the beginning of modern times. By leaving the Christian narrative of the Middle Ages behind, the radical orientation towards certainty *risks something new*. Enlightenment is also a narrative. Kant's moral theory, likewise, is a very risky narrative in which a moral God ensures that happiness is 'distributed in exact proportion to morality'.[5] God compensates us for our renunciation of earthly pleasures and pursuit of virtue. Kant's postulate of the soul's immortality is also a risky narrative. The 'production of the highest good', Kant argues, is 'possible only on the presupposition of the existence and personality of the same rational being continuing endlessly', because 'the complete conformity of dispositions with the moral law' is 'a perfection of which no rational being of the sensible world is capable at any moment of his existence'. That is, Kant postulates an 'endless progress' in which the human being, even beyond death, seeks to achieve the 'highest good'.[6] As far as the immortality of the soul is concerned, Kant's moral theory, *as a tale*, does not fundamentally differ from Plato's *myth*. But unlike Kant, Plato explicitly emphasizes that it is a narrative (*mythos*).

New narratives allow for new forms of perception. Nietzsche's revaluation of all values opens up a new perspective on the world. The world is, so to speak, *re-narrated*, and as a result we see it with fresh eyes. Nietzsche's *The Gay Science* is anything but a science in the narrow sense. It is conceived as a *narrative about the future* that is based on a 'hope', on a 'faith in a tomorrow and a day after tomorrow'. Nietzsche's revaluation of all values is a *narrative as risk and festival*, even as *adventure*. In the preface to *The Gay Science*, Nietzsche writes:

'Gay Science': this signifies the saturnalia of a mind that has patiently resisted a terrible, long pressure – patiently, severely, coldly, without yielding, but also without hope – and is now all of a sudden attacked by hope, by hope for health, by the *intoxication* of recovery. Is it any wonder that in the process much that is unreasonable and foolish comes to light, much wanton tenderness, lavished even on problems that have a prickly hide, not made to be fondled and lured? This entire book is really nothing but an amusement after long privation and powerlessness, the jubilation of returning strength, of a reawakened faith in a tomorrow and a day after tomorrow, of a sudden sense and anticipation of a future, of impending adventures, of reopened seas, of goals that are permitted and believed in again.[7]

Nietzsche, the narrator, specifically emphasizes his *authorship*: 'I have it in my hands, I have a hand for *switching perspectives*: which is why, for me alone, the *revaluation of values* was possible at all.'[8] Only to the extent that a theory is also a narrative can it be a *passion*. It is precisely because artificial intelligence is incapable of *passion*, of *passionate narration*, that it cannot think.

Once philosophy claims to be a science, an exact science even, decay sets in. Conceived as a science, philosophy denies its original narrative character and it loses its *language*. Philosophy *falls silent*. An academic philosophy that limits itself to the administration of its own history is unable to *narrate*. It does not run any *risks*; it runs a *bureaucracy*. The current crisis of narration thus also takes hold of philosophy and puts an end to it. We *lack* the courage for philosophy, the courage for theory, that is, *the courage to create a narrative*. We must always bear in mind that, in the final analysis, thinking is also a narrating that progresses in narrative steps.

Narration as Healing

In one of his 'thought figures', Walter Benjamin invokes the primordial scene of healing: 'The child is sick. His mother puts him to bed and sits down beside him. And then she begins to tell him stories.' Telling stories is healing because it creates deep relaxation and primordial trust. The loving voice of the mother soothes the child, strokes the child's soul, strengthens their bond, supports the child. Children's stories, moreover, tell of an ideal world; they turn the world into a familiar home. A standard children's story plot line relates the happy overcoming of a crisis. This helps the child to get over the crisis that the illness represents.

The hand that *narrates* is also healing. Benjamin speaks of the 'strange healing powers' that emanate from the woman's hands, which move as if telling of something: 'Their movements are highly expressive. But it is not possible to describe their expression ... It is as if they were telling a story.' Every illness is the sign of an inner blockage that can be released through the *rhythm of narration*. The *hand that tells a story* releases tension, blockages and hardenings. It puts things back into balance, even lets them *flow* again. Benjamin wonders 'whether every illness might be cured if it could only float along the river of narrative – until it reached the mouth'. Pain is a dam that offers an initial resistance to the narrative flow. But the narrative flow swells and eventually becomes strong enough to break the dam. Then, the flow takes with it everything along the way to the 'ocean of blissful oblivion'. The stroking hand 'marks out a bed for this torrent'. Benjamin points out 'that the story a sick man tells the doctor at the start of his treatment can become the first stage in the healing process'.[1]

Freud, too, understands pain as a symptom of a blockage in a person's history. The person is unable to continue their story. Psychological disorders are symptoms of a blocked story. The healing consists in the liberation of the patient from this narrative block, in bringing what cannot be narrated to linguistic expression. The patient is cured the moment she *narrates herself free*.

Narratives develop healing powers. Benjamin mentions the Merseburg charms, the second of which was intended as a magical healing procedure. It is not, however, an abstract formula. Rather, it tells the story of a wounded horse and Wotan's use of a magic spell. Benjamin notes: 'It is not simply that they repeat Wotan's formula; in addition, they *narrate* the situation which led him to use it in the first place.'[2]

A traumatic experience can be overcome by integrating it into a religious narrative that provides consolation or hope and thus carries us through the crisis. *Crisis narratives* help us to come to terms with catastrophic events by embedding them in meaningful contexts. Conspiracy theories also have a therapeutic function. They offer simple explanations for the complex situations that are responsible for crises. Conspiracy theories are therefore stories mostly told in times of crisis. When crisis threatens, *narration per se* has a therapeutic effect, because it *places the situation in the past*. As part of the past, it no longer affects the present. The situation is *put to bed*, so to speak.

Hannah Arendt prefaces the chapter on action in *The Human Condition* with an unusual line from Isak Dinesen: 'All sorrows can be borne if you put them into a story or tell a story about them.'[3] *Narrative phantasy* is healing. By placing our sorrows under the narrative light, it takes away their oppressive facticity. They are absorbed by narrative rhythms and melodies. A story raises them above mere facticity. Instead of solidifying into a mental block, they liquefy in the narrative flow.

Today's storytelling cannot prevent the disappearance of the *narrative atmosphere*. At doctors' surgeries, scarcely a story is told. Doctors have neither the time nor the patience to listen. The *spirit of narration* does not fit with the logic of efficiency. Only in psychotherapy and psychoanalysis are there still moments reminiscent of the healing powers of storytelling. Michael Ende's character Momo is able to heal people simply by listening to them. She has plenty of time: 'Time was Momo's only form of wealth.'[4] She gives her time to the other. The *time of the other* is a *good time*. Momo is the ideal listener:

No, what Momo was better at than anyone else was *listening*. Anyone can listen, you may say – what's so special about that? – but you'd be wrong. Very few people know how to listen properly, and Momo's way of listening was quite unique.[5]

Momo's friendly, attentive silence invokes in others ideas that would otherwise never have occurred to them:

It wasn't that she actually said anything or asked questions that put such ideas into their heads. She simply sat there and listened with utmost attention and sympathy, fixing them with her big, dark eyes, and they suddenly became aware of ideas they had never suspected.[6]

Momo allows others to *narrate themselves free*. She heals by removing narrative blockages:

Another time, a little boy brought her his canary because it wouldn't sing. Momo found that a far harder proposition. She had to sit and listen to the bird for a whole week before it started to trill and warble again.[7]

Listening is in the first instance directed at the other *person*, the *who of the other*, not at the content that is communicated. Momo's deep and friendly gaze *addresses* the others explicitly in their *otherness*. Listening is not a passive state; it is an active doing. *It inspires the other to narrate* and opens up a *resonating space* in which the narrator feels *addressed*, *heard*, even *loved*.

Touch also has healing powers. Like storytelling, touching creates closeness and primordial trust. As a *tactile narrative*, a touch releases tensions and blockages that lead to pain and illness. The physician Viktor von Weizsäcker invokes a primordial scene of healing:

> When a sister, still very young herself, sees her little brother in pain, she senses what to do before knowing anything: her hand finds its way; she wants to caress him where it hurts – *thus, the little Samaritan becomes the first doctor*. A pre-knowledge about a primal effect is unconsciously at work in her. That knowledge guides her urge towards her hand and leads the hand to perform the soothing caress. For that is what the brother will experience; the hand will soothe him. Between himself and the pain slips the sensation of being touched by the sisterly hand, and the pain retreats before this new sensation.[8]

The hand that touches has the same healing powers as the voice that narrates. It creates closeness and trust. It releases tension and removes fear.

We currently live in a society in which there is no touching. Touching someone presupposes the *otherness of the other*, which places them beyond simple availability. We cannot touch a consumable object – we take hold of it or take it into our possession. In particular, the smartphone, the embodiment of the digital dispositif, creates the illusion of universal availability. Its consumerist habitus takes hold in every sphere of life. It robs others of their otherness and reduces them to consumable objects.

The retreat of touch is making us ill. Lacking touch, we remain hopelessly entrapped in our ego. Touch in the proper sense pulls us out of our ego. Poverty in touch ultimately means poverty in world. It makes us depressive, lonely and fearful. Digitalization intensifies this poverty in touch and world. Paradoxically, the rise of connectivity separates us. That is the hopeless dialectic of connection. Being connected is not the same thing as being united.

'Stories' on social media, which are in fact mere self-promotion, separate people from each other. Unlike narratives, they produce neither closeness nor empathy. In the end, they are information adorned with images – information that is briefly registered and then disappears. The stories do not narrate; they *advertise*. Vying for attention does not create community. In the age of storytelling as storyselling, narration and advertisement become indistinguishable. That is the current crisis of narration.

Narrative Community

In his essay *Behutsame Ortsbestimmung* [A careful definition of a place], Péter Nádas describes a village with an
ancient wild pear tree at its centre. On warm summer
nights, the villagers meet under the tree and tell each
other stories. The village is a narrative community. The
stories, with the values and norms they carry, unite the
people. The narrative community is a community *without
communication*: 'You get the feeling that life here does not
consist of personal experiences . . . but of a deep keeping
of silence.'[1] Under the pear tree, the villagers indulge in
'ritual contemplation', a ritual silence, and give their bless-
ings to the 'content of collective consciousness': 'They do
not have opinions on this or that, but incessantly tell just
one great story.'[2] At the end of his essay, Nádas, not without some regret, writes: 'On warm summer nights, quiet
singing could be heard from under the wild pear tree.

The villagers sang quietly.... Today, there are no chosen trees, and the song of the village has faded.'³

In Nádas's narrative community, a community without communication, there is a silence, a silent unity. It is the exact opposite of today's information society. We no longer tell each other stories. Instead, we *communicate* incessantly. We *post*, *share* and *like*. The 'ritual contemplation' that blesses the content of collective consciousness gives way to the intoxication of communication and information. The noise of communication silences the song in which all villagers join, the *one great story* that unites them. *Community without communication gives way to communication without community.*

Stories create social cohesion. They offer meaning and bear values that create community. They must be distinguished from those narratives that found *a regime*. The narratives on which the neoliberal regime is based prevent the formation of community. The neoliberal narrative of performance turns every individual into an *entrepreneur of his own self*. Everyone competes with everyone else. The performance narrative does not produce social cohesion – it does not produce a *we*. On the contrary, it destroys solidarity and empathy. By separating individuals from one another, the neoliberal narratives of self-optimization, self-realization and authenticity destabilize society. When everyone worships the self, is a priest of themselves, when *everyone plays to the gallery, gives a performance of themselves*, no stable community can form.

Myths are *ritually staged shared narratives*.

However, not all narrative communities are myth-based communities that involve a shared collective consciousness. On the basis of narratives about the future, modern societies can create *dynamic narrative communities* that allow for change. Conservative and nationalist narratives that are directed against liberal permissiveness are exclusionary and discriminatory. But not all community-founding narratives are based on the *exclusion of the other*. There are also *inclusive narratives* that do not cling to a particular identity. For example, the radical universalism of Kant's philosophical sketch *Perpetual Peace* amounts to a master narrative in which all human beings and nations are included and united in a world community. Kant bases perpetual peace on the ideas of 'cosmopolitan right' and 'universal hospitality'.[4] According to these ideas,

> all men are entitled to present themselves in the society of others by virtue of their right to communal possession of the earth's surface. Since the earth is a globe, they cannot disperse over an infinite area, but must necessarily tolerate one another's company. And no-one originally has any greater right than anyone else to occupy any particular portion of the earth.[5]

In this universalist narrative, there can be no refugees. Every human being enjoys unlimited hospitality. Everyone is a cosmopolitan. Novalis is another thinker who argues for a radical universalism. He imagines a 'world family' beyond nation or identity. He takes poetry to be the medium of reconciliation and love. Poetry unites people and things in the most intimate community:

> Poetry elevates each single thing through a particular combination with the rest of the whole . . . poetry shapes

the beautiful society – the world family – the beautiful household of the universe. . . . The individual lives in the whole and the whole in the individual. Through poetry there arises the highest sympathy and common activity, the most intimate communion of the finite and the infinite.[6]

This most intimate community is a *narrative community*, but it rejects exclusionary narratives of identity.

Because we lack sufficiently strong communal narratives, our late modern societies are unstable. Without a shared narrative, the *political*, which makes *shared action* possible, cannot properly form. In the neoliberal regime, the shared narrative gradually disintegrates into *private narratives, models of self-realization*. The neoliberal regime prevents the formation of community-founding narratives. In the name of performance and productivity, it separates human beings from one another. As a result, we have few narratives that could serve to found community and meaning. The proliferation of private narratives erodes community. Stories on social media, which make the private public, undermine the *political public sphere* and make the formation of shared narratives even more difficult.

Political action in the genuine sense presupposes a narrative. The action must be *narratable*. Without a narrative, action deteriorates into contingent acts or reactions. Political action presupposes *narrative coherence*. Hannah Arendt explicitly links action to narration:

For action and speech, which, as we saw before, belonged close together in the Greek understanding of politics, are indeed the two activities whose end result will always be a story with enough coherence to be told, no matter how accidental or haphazard the single events and their causation may appear to be.[7]

Today, narratives are becoming more and more depoliticized. They mainly serve to create a society based on singularities – cultural singularities such as singular objects, styles, places, collectives or products.[8] As a consequence, they are no longer a force that forms community. Shared action, the *we*, is based on narrative. Narratives now mainly serve commercial interests. Storytelling as storyselling creates not a narrative community but a consumer society. Narratives are produced and consumed like commodities. Consumers do not form a community, a *we*. The commercialization of narratives robs them of their political force. When certain goods are embellished with moral narratives such as 'fair trade', even morality becomes consumable. The moral narrative becomes information, and is sold and consumed as a product's distinguishing feature. Moral consumption, mediated by narratives, increases only our own sense of self-worth. Through these narratives, we refer not to a community that is to be improved, but only to our own egos.

Storyselling

Storytelling is in vogue. Such is its popularity that it might seem as though we have a renewed passion for telling each other stories. In fact, however, this storytelling is anything but the return of narration. Instead, it serves to instrumentalize and commercialize narration. Storytelling is becoming established as an efficient *communication technology*, one that is often manipulative and has an ulterior motive. The question is always the same: 'How do we best use storytelling?' We would be mistaken to assume that all the product managers' chatter about storytelling indicates they are a new avant-garde promoting a genuine narrative.

Storytelling as storyselling does not have the force that characterizes genuine narration. Narratives introduce joints into being, so to speak. These give it orientation and support. As products of storytelling, by contrast, narratives share many features with information: they are ephemeral, contingent and consumable. They cannot stabilize life.

Narratives are more effective than bare facts or figures because they trigger emotions. Emotions are, in the main, responses to narratives. 'Stories sell' means, in effect, 'emotions sell'. Emotions are located in the limbic system, the part of our brain that controls our actions at the physical-instinctual level of which we are not conscious. Emotions can bypass our *intellect* and influence our behaviour. Our conscious defensive responses are thus circumvented. By intentionally appropriating narratives, capitalism takes hold of life at a pre-reflexive level and thus escapes conscious control and critical reflection.

Storytelling is spreading to different areas. Even data analysts are learning how to tell stories, on the grounds that data by themselves are soulless. Data are opposed to narrative. They do not touch people. They appeal to the understanding rather than the emotions. Budding journalists attend storytelling seminars, as if their task was to write novels. Most crucially, however, storytelling is used in marketing, where it is employed to transform even useless things into valuable goods. Critical for 'value added' is a narrative that promises customers something special. In the age of storytelling, we consume more narratives than things. Narrative content is more important than use value. Storytelling also commercializes the specific history of various places, whose history is commercially exploited to increase the value of the products that are produced there. A story [*Geschichte*] in the proper sense, by contrast, creates a *community* by giving it an identity. Storytelling turns every story [*Geschichte*] into a commodity.[1]

Even politicians have cottoned on to the fact that *stories sell*. In the battle for attention, narratives are more effective than arguments. They are therefore instrumentalized in politics. Politicians address the emotions, not the intellect. When used as a political communication technique, storytelling does not convey a *political vision* that reaches into the future and provides meaning and orientation. Genuine political narratives open up a perspective on a new order of things; they paint pictures of *possible* worlds. Today, we singularly lack such hopeful *narratives of the future*. We lurch from one crisis to the next. Politics is reduced to problem solving. Only narratives open up a future.

Living is narrating. The human being is an *animal narrans*, and differs from animals to the extent that, through narrative, new forms of life are brought about. A narrative contains the *power of a new beginning*. Every action that changes the world presupposes a narrative. But storytelling knows only one form of life, and that is life as consumption. Storytelling as storyselling is incapable of designing substantially different forms of life. In the world of storytelling, everything is reduced to consumption. This blinds us to other stories, other forms of life, to other perceptions and realities. Therein lies the crisis of narration in the age of storytelling.

Notes

Preface

1 Transl. note: Here and throughout, 'storytelling' is in English in the original, except in passages on Walter Benjamin, where the German is 'Erzähler'/'Erzählen'. The term is used for commodified forms of narration, as opposed to the proper telling of stories, 'Geschichten erzählen'. The term 'storytelling' should therefore not be associated with Walter Benjamin's well-known essay 'The Storyteller', 'Der Erzähler', which spells out the characteristics of the proper telling of stories.

2 Niklas Luhmann, 'Entscheidungen in der Informationsgesellschaft', at https://www.fen.ch/texte/gast_luhmann_informationsgesellschaft.htm

From Narration to Information

1 All quotations from Walter Benjamin, 'The Storyteller: Observations on the Works of Nikolai Leskov', in *Selected*

Writings, Vol. 3, 1935–1938, Cambridge MA: Harvard University Press, 2002, pp. 143–66; here: p. 147.

2 Ibid., p. 148.

3 Ibid.

4 Walter Benjamin, *The Arcades Project*, Cambridge MA: Harvard University Press, 1999, p. 447.

5 Benjamin, 'The Storyteller', p. 147.

6 Ibid., pp. 147f.

7 Ibid., p. 148. Benjamin does not quote from Psammenitus's story verbatim. The original differs significantly from his summary. It seems that he follows the version presented by Michel de Montaigne in the *Essais*.

8 Ibid.

9 Ibid., p. 146.

10 Ibid., p. 147 (transl. modified).

11 Ibid., p. 149.

12 Benjamin, *The Arcades Project*, p. 105.

13 Benjamin, 'The Storyteller', p. 149. Transl. note: 'Rustling in the leaves' translates 'Rauschen im Blätterwald'. 'Blätterwald' is a colloquial and mildly dismissive term for the growing number of press titles whose quantity is not necessarily matched by their quality.

14 Benjamin, 'The Storyteller', p. 149.

15 Georg Büchner, *Danton's Death*, Act 2, Scene 5, in *The Major Works*, New York: W. W. Norton, 2012, p. 52.

The Poverty of Experience

1 Walter Benjamin, 'Experience and Poverty', in *Selected Writings, Vol. 2, Part 2 (1931–1934)*, Cambridge MA: Harvard University Press, 1999, pp. 731–6; here: p. 731.

2 Benjamin, 'The Storyteller', p. 145 (transl. modified).

3 Ibid., p. 146.

4 Ibid.

5 Benjamin, 'Experience and Poverty', pp. 731f.

6 Ibid., p. 732
7 Ibid.
8 Ibid., p. 734.
9 Ibid., p. 733.
10 Ibid.
11 Ibid., pp. 733f.
12 Ibid., pp. 734f.
13 Ibid., p. 735 (transl. modified).
14 Ibid.
15 Paul Scheerbart, *Glass Architecture*, in *Paul Scheerbart, 'Glass Architecture' and Bruno Taut, 'Alpine Architecture'*, New York: Praeger, 1972, pp. 41–74; here: p. 46.
16 Ibid. (transl. modified).
17 Karl Marx and Frederick Engels, *Manifesto of the Communist Party*, in *Economic and Philosophic Manuscripts of 1844 and The Communist Manifesto*, New York: Prometheus Books, 1988, pp. 203–43; here: p. 243.
18 Bertolt Brecht, *Plays, Poetry and Prose: Journals 1934–1955*, New York: Routledge, 1993, p. 166 (22 October 1941).

The Narrated Life

1 Benjamin, *The Arcades Project*, p. 479.
2 Marcel Proust, *In Search of Lost Time, Vol. VI: Time Regained*, London: Vintage, 1996, p. 451.
3 Ibid.
4 Ibid.
5 Martin Heidegger, *Being and Time*, Oxford: Blackwell, 1962, p. 442.
6 Ibid., p. 427.
7 Ibid., p. 442.
8 Ibid., p. 426.
9 Ibid., p. 435.
10 Walter Benjamin, 'The Work of Art in the Age of

Its Technological Reproducibility', in *Selected Writings*, *Vol. 3*, pp. 101–33; here: p. 117.

11 See Byung-Chul Han, *Psychopolitics: Neoliberalism and New Technologies of Power*, London: Verso, 2017.

Bare Life

1 Jean-Paul Sartre, *Nausea*, Norfolk CT: New Directions, 1949, p. 30.

2 Ibid., p. 20.

3 Ibid., p. 41.

4 Ibid., p. 116 (transl. amended).

5 Ibid., p. 19.

6 Ibid., p. 56.

7 Ibid., p. 57.

8 Ibid., p. 238.

9 Peter Handke, 'Essay on the Jukebox', in *The Jukebox and Other Essays on Storytelling*, New York: Farrar, Straus and Giroux, 1994, pp. 47–118; here: p. 48 (transl. modified).

10 Ibid., pp. 83f.

11 Jean Baudrillard, *Das Andere selbst*, Vienna: Passagen, 1994, p. 19.

The Disenchantment of the World

1 Paul Maar, 'Die Geschichte vom Jungen, der keine Geschichten erzählen konnte', in *Die Zeit*, 28 October 2004.

2 Novalis (Friedrich von Hardenberg), 'The Disciples at Saïs', in *The Disciples at Saïs and Other Fragments*, London: Methuen, 1903, pp. 91–143; here p. 129 (transl. modified).

3 Walter Benjamin, 'One-Way Street', in *Selected Writings*, *Vol. 1, 1913–1926*, Cambridge MA: Harvard University Press, pp. 444–88; here: pp. 465f.

4 Walter Benjamin, 'On Some Motifs in Baudelaire', in

Selected Writings, Vol. 4, 1938–1940, Cambridge MA: Harvard University Press, 2003, pp. 313–55; here: p. 338.

5 See Siegfried Kracauer, *The Mass Ornament: Weimar Essays*, Cambridge MA: Harvard University Press, 1995, pp. 50f.

6 See Proust, *Time Regained*, p. 241: 'Certain people, whose minds are prone to mystery, like to believe that objects retain something of the eyes which have looked at them, that old buildings and pictures appear to us not as they originally were but beneath a perceptible veil woven for them over the centuries by the love and contemplation of millions of admirers.'

7 Benjamin, *The Arcades Project*, p. 314 (transl. amended).

8 Benjamin, 'On Some Motifs in Baudelaire', p. 338.

9 Proust, *Time Regained*, p. 241.

10 Benjamin, 'On Some Motifs in Baudelaire', p. 354 (note 77).

11 Paul Virilio, *The Information Bomb*, London: Verso, 2005, p. 38.

12 Susan Sontag, 'At the Same Time: The Novelist and Moral Reasoning', in *At the Same Time: Essays and Speeches*, New York: Farrar, Straus and Giroux, 2007, pp. 210–31; here: p. 224.

13 Ibid.

14 Paul Virilio, 'Cyberwar, God and Television: An Interview with Paul Virilio', in Arthur and Marilouise Kroker (eds), *Digital Delirium*, Montreal: New World Perspectives, 1997, pp. 41–8; here: p. 47.

15 Gershom Scholem, *Major Trends in Jewish Mysticism*, New York: Schocken, 1995 [1946], pp. 349f.

16 Theodor W. Adorno, 'Gruß an G. Scholem. Zum 70. Geburtstag', in *Gesammelte Schriften Vol. 20.2*, Frankfurt am Main: Suhrkamp, 1997, pp. 478–86.

1 Benjamin, 'On Some Motifs in Baudelaire', p. 342.

2 Ibid., p. 343.

3 Benjamin, 'The Work of Art in the Age of Its Technological Reproducibility', p. 281 (note 42).

4 Benjamin, 'On Some Motifs in Baudelaire', p. 317.

5 Ibid., p. 341.

6 Ibid., p. 319.

7 Jacques Lacan, *The Four Fundamental Concepts of Psychoanalysis: The Seminar of Jacques Lacan, Book XI*, New York: W. W. Norton, 1998 [1973], p. 101.

8 Martin Heidegger, 'The Origin of the Work of Art', in *Off the Beaten Track*, Cambridge: Cambridge University Press, 2002, pp. 1–56; here: p. 10.

9 Sigmund Freud, *Beyond the Pleasure Principle*, New York: W. W. Norton, 1961, p. 21.

Theory as Narrative

1 Chris Anderson, 'The End of Theory: The Data Deluge Makes the Scientific Method Obsolete', *Wired*, 23 July 2008, at https://www.wired.com/2008/06/pb-theory

2 Elisabeth Bronfen: 'Theory as Narrative: Sigmund Freud', in Dieter Mersch, Silvia Sasse and Sandro Zanetti (eds), *Aesthetic Theory*, Zurich: Diaphanes, 2019, pp. 53–68; here: p. 55.

3 Plato, *Phaedo*, in *Complete Works*, Indianapolis: Hackett, 1997, pp. 49–100; here: p. 96 (113e).

4 Ibid., p. 97 (114d).

5 Immanuel Kant, *Critique of Practical Reason*, Cambridge: Cambridge University Press, 2015, p. 90.

6 Ibid., pp. 98f.

7 Friedrich Nietzsche, *The Gay Science*, Cambridge: Cambridge University Press, 2001, p. 3.

8 Friedrich Nietzsche, *Nachgelassene Fragmente 1887–1889*,

Kritische Studienausgabe, Vol. 13, Berlin: de Gruyter, 1988, p. 630. Transl. note: See the almost, but not quite, identical wording in *Ecce Homo* (*The Anti-Christ, Ecce Homo, Twilight of the Idols, and Other Writings*, Cambridge: Cambridge University Press, 2005, p. 76): 'I have a hand for switching perspectives: the first reason why a "revaluation of values" is even possible, perhaps for me alone.' The English translation of *Ecce Homo* leaves out 'Ich habe es jetzt in der Hand' [I now have it in my hands, . . .]. Note the addition of 'now' (*jetzt*) and the change from past to present tense ('was' to 'is' possible).

Narration as Healing

1 All quotations from Walter Benjamin, 'Storytelling and Healing', in *Selected Writings, Vol. 2, Part 2*, pp. 724f.
2 Ibid. (transl. amended; emphasis B.-C. Han).
3 Hannah Arendt, *The Human Condition*, Chicago: Chicago University Press, 1998 [1958], p. 175. Transl. note: The quotation is from an interview with Karen Blixen conducted by Bent Mohn ('Talk with Isak Dinesen', *The New York Times Book Review*, 3 November 1957): 'I am not a novelist, really not even a writer; I am a storyteller. One of my friends said about me that I think all sorrows can be borne if you put them into a story or tell a story about them, and perhaps this is not entirely untrue. To me, the explanation of life seems to be its melody, its pattern. And I feel in life such an infinite, truly inconceivable fantasy.' Karen Blixen and Isak Dinesen are two pen names of Karen Christenze von Blixen-Finecke.
4 Michael Ende, *Momo*, New York: Doubleday & Company Inc., 1985, p. 12.
5 Ibid., p. 11.
6 Ibid.
7 Ibid., pp. 15f.

8 Viktor von Weizsäcker, 'Die Schmerzen', in *Der Arzt und der Kranke: Stücke einer medizinischen Anthropologie*, Gesammelte Schriften, Vol. 5, Frankfurt am Main: Suhrkamp, 1987, pp. 27–47; here p. 27.

Narrative Community

1 Péter Nádas, *Behutsame Ortsbestimmung: Zwei Berichte*, Berlin: Berlin Verlag, 2006, p. 11. Transl. note: The German book contains two texts, 'Genaue Ortsbestimmung' and 'Der eigene Tod', originally published separately in Hungarian: 'A helyzsin óvatos megházozása' (A careful definition of a place), in *Hátországi napló: Újabb usszék* (Diary from the hinterland: recent essays), Pécs: Jelenkor, 2006, and *Saját halál* (One's own death), Pécs: Jelenkor, 2004.

2 Nádas, *Behutsame Ortsbestimmung*, p. 25 and p. 17.

3 Ibid., p. 33.

4 Immanuel Kant, *Perpetual Peace: A Philosophical Sketch*, Cambridge: Cambridge University Press, 1991, pp. 93–130; here: p. 105.

5 Ibid., p. 106.

6 Novalis (Friedrich von Hardenberg), *Philosophical Writings*, New York: State University of New York, 1997, p. 54.

7 Arendt, *The Human Condition*, p. 97.

8 See Andreas Reckwitz, *The Society of Singularities*, Cambridge: Polity, 2020.

Storyselling

1 Transl. note: In the German, 'Geschichte' can mean both 'story' and 'history'.